for beginners

AI in Finance for Beginners

Explore the Applications of AI in Algorithmic Trading, Fraud Detection, and Financial Forecasting

Printed in the United States of America

First Edition: 2025

This copyright page includes the necessary copyright notice, permissions request information, acknowledgments for the cover design, interior design, and editing, as well as the details of the first edition.

www.littlebiggiant.com

Disclaimer: This book is a work of non-fiction and is intended for informational and educational purposes only. The names in this biography are trademarks of their respective owners. This book is not affiliated with, endorsed by, or sponsored by any of these trademark holders. The use of these names is intended solely to provide context and historical reference.

The author makes no claims to ownership of any trademarks or copyrights associated with the names and likenesses of the individuals referenced in this book. Any opinions expressed in this book are those of the author and do not reflect the views of any wrestling promotion or trademark holder.

Introduction

Screens blinked. Numbers jumped like nervous frogs. A young analyst stared at a wall of charts and felt the room tilt. Trades kept happening faster than any human hand could move. Machines were buying and selling in tiny slices. The air smelled faintly of coffee and worry.

A short headline from 2017 suddenly felt close enough to touch: a big bank used an AI program to read loan documents in seconds and saved about 360,000 hours of work. That was not a story far away. It was a proof that lines of code can do real, heavy tasks in finance. Algorithms now run much of the buying and selling. They hunt for fraud. They guess what might happen next in markets. The analyst whispered, "This is out of control." Inside, a question pulsed: What happens if the machine is wrong?

Some beats were quick and sharp. Screens flashed green. A red alert pinged. Confusion tightened like a knot. Fear felt honest and small, but so did the person pressing the keys. Machines can make mistakes. People can fix them. Machines can spot stolen cards by patterns humans miss. Machines can test a thousand possible futures in minutes. That is both terrifying and hopeful.

The moment held two truths: technology moves faster than nerves, and understanding it changes the story. Algorithms already watch for fake transactions. Models already try to forecast prices from weather reports, news, and lots of tiny clues. Yet those same tools can be tools for everyone who learns them—not just the suited traders on the screen.

So which side will curiosity pick? Will the machines stay mysterious and frightening, or will the next reader learn the rules and tips that make them useful and safe? The room waited. The screen waited. The next step could be a rescue, or a mistake — and the answer starts with a single, careful question: how does AI actually do its work in finance?

Table of Contents

Chapter 1

Foundations of AI and Finance

By the end of this chapter, you will understand the core AI ideas used in finance, the main types of financial data you'll work with, and the basic tools that help you turn data into insights.

Overview of AI concepts relevant to financial applications

In finance, AI is a way to turn data into smarter decisions. At a high level, AI means teaching computers to spot patterns, make predictions, or choose actions based on what they have seen before. Machine learning is a common approach inside AI. It means the computer learns from examples rather than following a fixed set of rules. For you, that often means looking at past data to guess what might happen next.

You don't need to be a genius programmer to start. The practical idea is simple: you collect data, you train a model on that data, you test whether it works on new data, and you keep watching it after you put it into use. A few big ideas help you stay on track. First, more data and better data usually beat fancy algorithms. Second, simple models are often easier to understand and safer to use in real life. Third, models are not magic. They reflect the data they were fed, so bad data leads to bad decisions. Fourth, keep a careful eye on leakage—when information from the future sneaks into your training data, your model will look smarter than it should and fail in the real world.

In practice, you'll often separate tasks into supervised and unsupervised learning. Supervised learning uses labeled examples—instances where you already know the answer. For example, you might train a model to decide if a trade was profitable or not based on past trades. Unsupervised learning looks for patterns without labeled outcomes. It helps you discover clusters of similar trades, unusual activity, or hidden relationships in data. A third flavor, reinforcement learning, is about learning by trying actions and seeing what happens. In finance, reinforcement ideas show up in how an agent might learn trading rules over time, but they require careful testing and safeguards.

A quick mental model helps. Think of AI as a collaborative system: you provide data and goals, the model suggests patterns, and you interpret and act on those patterns. The human in the loop remains essential for setting objectives, checking for bias, and keeping things safe. In all cases, you document assumptions, monitor performance, and adjust as markets change.

Two practical anchor points you'll use constantly are features and evaluation. Features are the measurements you feed to a model. They could be numbers like prices, volumes, or ratios you compute from raw data. Evaluation is how you judge whether the model is doing a good job. In finance, evaluation often means comparing the model's predictions to actual outcomes, watching for overfitting, and ensuring the model behaves reasonably in new situations.

In short, AI in finance is about turning data into better questions, clearer signals, and safer decisions. You start with simple goals, keep your data clean, test carefully, and build a process you can repeat. That steady workflow—data, model, test, monitor—will carry you through many chapters as you go deeper.

Types of financial data and common data pipelines

Finance produces many kinds of data, all with different shapes and stories. Price data is a common starting point. It records the price of an asset over time and often includes the opening price, closing price, high, low, and traded volume for each time interval. Time is the key dimension here; you align data by timestamps so you can compare what happened at the same moments across different assets or markets.

Transaction data is another big category. It captures individual buys and sells, often with details like amount, counterpart, location, and time. This data helps you study behavior, detect unusual activity, and measure risk. Then there's order book data, which shows the current supply and demand at different price levels. It's like watching the heartbeat of a market as traders place bids and asks.

Macro and contextual data round out the picture. You might see indicators such as economic reports, interest rates, or company news. Alternative data—non-traditional sources like weather, satellite imagery, or social sentiment—can also add flavour, though you treat it the same way as other data: with care, because quality matters.

A data pipeline is the path data travels from collection to decision. First comes data collection: you pull data from places like price feeds, trade logs, or economic releases. Second is data cleaning: you check for duplicates, fix obvious errors, and remove obviously wrong values. Third is data alignment and integration: you bring different sources onto a common timeline, so a price value lines up with the right transaction or news item. Fourth is feature extraction and transformation:

you compute new numbers that help a model see patterns—moving averages, rate of change, volatility measures, or simple ratios. Fifth is storage and access: you save data in a way that makes it easy to retrieve for training and testing. Finally, you may have real-time or near-real-time streaming, where data flows in continuously, or batch processing, where you update things at regular intervals.

Three practical notes show how this plays out. First, start with clean, well-documented data. If you cannot explain where a value came from or how it was computed, treat it with suspicion. Second, align data by time. Markets move fast, and misaligned timestamps are a common source of errors that look like clever insights. Third, test everything on fresh data. A model might seem amazing on yesterday's data but stumble on today's reality.

Two short micro-cases illustrate the point. Case A: You want to forecast a stock's next-day return using a simple set of past prices. You gather minute-by-minute prices for the last 20 sessions, compute a small set of features like the average of the past 5 minutes and the ratio of the last price to the 20-minute average, and you train a basic linear model to predict the sign of the return. The goal is not to become a market oracle but to create a signal you can monitor. If the model's predictions align with actual moves better than random chance, that's your cue to keep the feature set simple and track performance over time.

Case B: You're trying to flag unusual transactions for review. You pull transaction data with amounts, times, and locations, and you compute a simple score based on how far an amount is from the typical daily average. When the score crosses a threshold, you flag it for human review. This teaches you the value of a fast, interpretable detector that can run in real time and be easily explained to others.

In practice, you will often combine several data streams. A compact, transparent pipeline might use price data and a small set of technical indicators, merged with basic transaction flags to help you understand where signals come from. You keep your pipeline modular so you can swap in better data or a different model without ripping the whole system apart.

Basic statistical and machine learning techniques used in finance

You begin with the fundamentals. Statistical thinking starts with numbers: the mean or average shows central tendency, while variance and standard deviation measure how spread out values are. A simple correlation tells you whether two variables move in the same direction. These ideas help you spot patterns and judge how strong a signal might be.

Moving from purely descriptive statistics to prediction, you'll use regression tools. Linear regression tries to fit a straight line to data and can estimate how much one variable changes when another one moves. In finance, a basic use is predicting a future value—like a price or return—based on past behavior and a few carefully chosen inputs. Logistic regression switches gears when you want to predict a probability—such as the chance that a transaction will be flagged as unusual—rather than a numeric value.

Time matters in finance, so you'll hear about time-series ideas. A simple moving average smooths out noise by averaging values over a window, helping you see trends. More advanced time-series models, like ARIMA, use patterns in past data to forecast future values. You don't need to master every model to start; the key is to understand the concept: use history to inform what might come next, while watching for signs that history is not predicting the future well.

Trees and ensembles offer another reliable route. A decision tree splits data into branches to predict outcomes, based on questions about features. Random forests and gradient boosting combine many trees to improve accuracy and resilience. These ideas are often easier to interpret than deep neural networks, which can be powerful but harder to explain to others who rely on your results.

Neural networks show up in finance too, especially when you work with complex patterns or large feature sets. A simple feedforward network can approximate relationships, while recurrent networks or transformers handle sequences, like price paths or event streams. In this book's early stage, you'll mainly see mentions of these tools as possibilities; the emphasis stays on understanding data, choosing transparent models when possible, and validating performance.

Two micro-cases help ground these ideas. Micro-case 1: You test a simple linear regression to predict next-day returns using a handful of past-return features. You measure success by how often your predicted direction matches the actual move and by whether your model adds value beyond a naive baseline (like "always predict no change"). If results are modest but stable across new data sets, you've built a credible, interpretable signal you can grow. Micro-case 2: You deploy a small anomaly detector using a threshold on a standardized feature, such as the z-score of transaction size. You watch for false positives and false negatives, adjust thresholds, and ensure the detector remains explainable to risk managers.

As you move from ideas to practice, keep these guardrails in mind. First, start small. Choose one data source, one target, and one straightforward model. Second, emphasize interpretability. In finance, being able to explain a signal helps you gain trust and to audit decisions later. Third, guard against leakage. Use only data available before the decision point when training. Fourth, validate with fresh data. A model that seems great on old data can fail in new conditions.

Three practical exercises to practice what you've learned. Exercise 1: Data types inventory. Take ten minutes to list five different kinds of financial data you might encounter (price, volume, transactions, order book, macro indicators). For each, write one sentence about its typical format and a simple question you could answer with it. Measure progress by the completeness and clarity of your list. Exercise 2: Build a tiny data-pipeline sketch. In fifteen minutes, outline a minimal workflow: where data comes from, what cleaning steps you'd perform, which two or three features you'd compute, and how you'd use the results to make a decision. Check progress by ensuring the pipeline maps cleanly from data source to action. Exercise 3: Simple statistics practice. Use a small five-number data sample (e.g., daily returns: -2, 0, 1, 3, -1). Compute the mean, median, and standard deviation. Explain in one sentence what each number tells you about the data. Measure progress by the clarity of your interpretation. Exercise 4: Model idea and rationale. Write one short paragraph proposing a simple model to predict a financial metric (like next-day return or flagging a transaction). Include the feature you'd use and a brief justification for why that feature matters. Time yourself for five minutes and review whether your idea is easy to explain to someone else.

A brief toolbox and templates you can copy. The data-world is full of tools, but you don't need a heavy setup to begin. Use a simple notebook or a familiar spreadsheet for small experiments. Think in terms of three templates: 1) Data source and quality checklist: what data are you using, how clean is it, and what checks do you perform before training? 2) Model intuition sheet: which model you try, what features it uses, and why you expect it to work? 3) Evaluation log: what metric will you track, what baseline are you comparing against, and how will you decide if you're done for now? These short templates help you stay organized as you grow.

Common pitfalls and quick fixes. A frequent snag is data leakage: you accidentally use information from the future to train your model. Fix by keeping a clear cut between training and testing data and by validating that all features are computed without peeking into future values. Another problem is overfitting, where your model captures noise instead of real signals. Fix with simpler models, more data, and proper cross-validation. If results look great only on one dataset but not others, re-check data quality and whether you've used the same data distribution in training and testing. Finally, beware bias or unfairness. If your signals reflect biased patterns, pause, re-express the problem, and include fairness checks in your evaluation.

Tools and templates you can reuse without heavy setup. A simple data-workflow checklist can be printed or saved as a note: Data sources, data quality checks, feature set, model choice, evaluation metric, cross-validation plan, and deployment guardrails. A one-page model idea sheet helps you capture the feature choices and the rationale in plain language for quick reviews with teammates. A short evaluation table lets you compare models side by side using a single, clear metric and a sanity check for interpretability.

Key Takeaway: Start with clear data, simple models, and honest evaluation; good signals come from clean data and careful testing, not from fancy tricks alone.

Coming up next: In the next chapter, you will learn how to clean, normalize, and enrich data for finance, build time-series features, and prevent leaks that can mislead your models. You'll also see how to construct reliable data pipelines so your early experiments turn into solid groundwork for real work. Coming up next, Data Preparation and Feature Engineering.

Chapter 2

Data Preparation and Feature Engineering

By the end of this chapter you will clean, normalize, and enrich financial data, build time-series and event-driven features, and handle missing data, class imbalance, and data leakage with practical, repeatable steps.

Cleaning, Normalizing, and Enriching Data

Step 1: Gather data from reliable sources and align formats

Collect data from multiple sources with care. You may pull price quotes, trade records, and market indicators, then bring them into one common format. The practical goal is a single, coherent view where each data point has a clear time stamp, a labeled source, and a consistent data type. If two sources use different date formats, you convert them so every row lines up on the same clock. Why this matters: alignment reduces gaps and misreads, so your models won't learn from mismatched signals.

Step 2: Clean obvious errors, duplicates, and outliers

Scan for obvious mistakes like negative prices, impossible timestamps, or repeated rows. Remove duplicates and outliers that don't reflect real market activity, or flag them for separate review. The core idea is to keep what reflects true activity and set aside what could mislead a model. Example: if one source shows a spark of price that's wildly off the market price for a moment, you might deem it suspect and set it aside for closer inspection.

Step 3: Normalize numeric values and standardize units

Make numeric fields comparable by scaling or standardizing where it helps. Convert currencies when needed, and bring all units to a common standard so a feature means the same thing everywhere. For example, if one dataset uses dollars and another uses euros, you normalize to a single currency or clearly tag the currency as a feature. Why: uniform units prevent the model from treating a currency difference as a real signal.

Step 4: Enrich data with helpful metadata

Add context that helps interpretation without changing the core numbers. This can include data provenance (where the data came from), timestamps in a consistent time zone, and simple quality flags (high confidence, questionable, missing). You can also create simple derived fields such as market session label (pre-market, regular, after-hours) or action types (buy, sell, hold) that help later steps understand the data's story. Why: metadata makes the data easier to audit and use correctly in modeling.

Step 5: Do quick quality checks and document your rules

Run basic checks to confirm the data looks sensible after cleaning and enrichment. Check row counts, time continuity, and known relationships (for instance, price and volume patterns should move together in reasonable ways). Document the rules you used—what you changed, why, and when you might revisit them. This makes your work auditable and repeatable.

Examples and micro-cases

Example 1: You have price data from two exchanges. You first align timestamps to a shared clock, remove duplicates, and then average prices when both exchanges report the same moment. The result is a clean, smooth price series with fewer glitches, ready for analysis.

Example 2: You're working with order data that arrives in separate files. You add a feature for "time since last trade" and a flag for whether a trade occurred during a volatile market period. You also tag records with a source so you can trace back if something looks odd. The enriched dataset helps you see patterns that raw numbers might miss.

Constructing Time-Series and Event-Driven Features

Step 1: Decide the right level of detail (granularity)

Choose how fine or broad your time steps should be (for example, daily, hourly, or per-minute). This choice depends on your goal and the data you have. Smaller steps give more detail but need more data and care for gaps; bigger steps are simpler and faster to check. The underlying principle is: be consistent, not chaotic, about the time axis.

Step 2: Align data streams to the same timeline

If you're bringing together prices, volumes, and event data, ensure they line up on the same timestamps. If one stream lags, you'll end up mixing signals from different moments, which can confuse a model. A practical fix is to resample or interpolate data to a common timeline, keeping only signals that exist at that moment.

Step 3: Create lagged features and moving statistics

Lag features look back at past values (for example, price one day ago, five days ago). Moving averages smooth noise and reveal trends (like a 20-day average). You can also calculate returns over different horizons (daily return, weekly return) to capture momentum and direction. The rationale is simple: finance signals often depend on what happened before, not just what's happening right now.

Step 4: Build rate-of-change and volatility indicators

Compute how fast prices move (rate of change) and how much they wiggle (volatility). These measures help you gauge risk and potential turning points. Use them as features to inform a model about when a market is calm or choppy, without replacing the primary signals with guesswork.

Step 5: Create event-driven features

Mark the calendar with events that tend to affect markets (economic announcements, earnings releases, policy meetings). Add binary indicators that an event is near or has occurred, and maybe a few days of post-event behavior. The goal is to let the model notice whether signals shift around events rather than assuming they behave the same every day.

Step 6: Synchronize diverse data streams

If you have multiple data types (prices, quotes, order books, sentiment feeds), synchronize them to the same cadence. This may require down-sampling or careful re-indexing. The point is to ensure the model sees aligned stories rather than mismatched fragments.

Step 7: Keep a feature catalog and sanity checks

Maintain a running list of features, what they represent, and any known limitations. Do quick sanity checks to confirm a feature behaves as intended (for example, a moving average should not be wildly unresponsive to real movement). This habit helps prevent late surprises during modeling.

Examples and micro-cases

Micro-case 1: You construct a 5-day and a 20-day moving average of closing prices. You also compute daily returns and a simple volatility estimate over 10 days. You find that the blend of short and long-term indicators helps you spot short-term momentum while suppressing random noise.

Micro-case 2: You pair stock prices with an event flag for quarterly earnings. You notice that near earnings, a surge in trading volume often coincides with price jumps. You layer an event-weighted feature that increases the signal strength around those dates, helping a forecasting model pick up event-driven patterns.

Addressing Missing Data, Class Imbalance, and Data Leakage

Step 1: Handle missing data with practical rules

Use straightforward approaches first. For numeric fields, you can fill gaps with the median or mean, or use forward filling for time-series data where appropriate. It's helpful to create a missingness indicator—an extra feature that says "was this value missing?"—so the model can learn whether missingness itself carries information. The aim is to keep data usable without making up numbers that mislead the model.

Step 2: Tackle class imbalance with sensible strategies

When some outcomes are rare (like a rare event in fraud detection or unusual price moves), you have a few practical choices. You can use methods that pay more attention to the minority class, adjust decision thresholds, or use resampling to balance the data. The goal is to make the model sensitive enough to the rare events without inflating false alarms. Remember: the right approach depends on your data and your goals, not on a single trick.

Step 3: Prevent data leakage before you start

Data leakage happens when information from the future leaks into the training data. This can happen if you mix data from future time points into your model's learning process. A simple rule: never use outcomes that wouldn't be known at the moment you're making a prediction. Keep a clean separation between training data and the data you'd actually use in live forecasting. If you're unsure, imagine you're predicting today's price based only on yesterday's and earlier information.

Step 4: Use time-aware validation to test your ideas

When you test ideas, use validation methods that respect the order of time. This means training on earlier periods and testing on later periods, not random shuffles. This approach mirrors real life, where you forecast with information you already have and see how it would have performed in a future window. The practice helps you measure true predictive power instead of an illusion created by random splits.

Step 5: Document your assumptions and checks

Keep notes about what you did and why. If you impute a missing value a certain way or decide to drop a sample because it leaks future information, write that down. Documentation makes it easier to repeat, audit, and improve your work as you learn more.

Examples and micro-cases

Micro-case 1: You have a fraud dataset with far fewer positive cases than negatives. You try balancing by slightly oversampling the positives and adjusting the model's decision threshold. You observe improved recall with a careful balance so you don't flood the system with false alarms. The key is to keep an eye on precision as you adjust.

Micro-case 2: You train a model with a rolling window that always uses past data. You keep a separate holdout period for final testing that mirrors real-time use. When you eventually deploy, you won't be surprised by a drift suddenly changing results because you tested with data that wouldn't be available at prediction time.

Key Takeaway: Clean data, thoughtful features, and careful handling of gaps and biases turn messy data into reliable signals you can trust.

Coming up next: Subtittle: Supervised and Unsupervised Methods for Finance

1) Regression, classification, and ensemble approaches for prediction,

2) Clustering and dimensionality reduction for segmentation,

3) Choosing between supervised and unsupervised workflows

Coming up next

Subtittle: Supervised and Unsupervised Methods for Finance

1) Regression, classification, and ensemble approaches for prediction,

2) Clustering and dimensionality reduction for segmentation,

3) Choosing between supervised and unsupervised workflows

Chapter 3

Supervised and Unsupervised Methods for Finance

By the end of this chapter, you will be able to choose appropriate supervised or unsupervised methods and apply them to financial data to make clearer predictions, useful groups, and smarter decisions.

Regression, classification, and ensemble approaches for prediction

You start by pairing the problem with the right learning task. If you want a numeric forecast, you use regression. If you want a category label—like "price will rise," "price will fall," or "no change"—you use classification. If you want better accuracy or robustness, you layer models together in an ensemble. Ensembles can be simple, like combining a few different models, or more complex, like stacking one model's output on top of another's. The goal is to reduce errors and capture different signals that individual models might miss.

Step 1: Define the target clearly. Decide if you need a precise number (next-day return, price, or volatility) or a direction or category (up/down/flat). The target shape guides every other choice, from features to evaluation metrics. Rationale: clarity here prevents you from building the wrong thing in the first place.

Step 2: Gather sensible features. Start with straightforward inputs: recent prices, moving averages, trading volume, and simple indicators. Include a few event-based features if you can (like earnings days or macro releases) but avoid overloading with too many variables at once. Rationale: useful features give models something to learn from without drowning them in noise.

Step 3: Build a simple baseline. For regression, a linear or ridge regression model provides a transparent starting point. For classification, logistic or simple decision-tree models are easy to interpret. Rationale: a transparent baseline shows you whether more complexity is truly needed and helps you understand what the signals look like.

Step 4: Add ensemble methods. If the baseline underperforms, try a forest of trees (random forest) or a boosted ensemble (gradient boosting). Ensemble methods often improve accuracy by blending different decision rules and reducing variance. Rationale: combining minds can smooth out mistakes that any single model makes.

Step 5: Split your data properly. Use a clean training set, a validation set to tune you parameters, and a final test set that you never touch during modeling. Avoid leakage from the future into training data. Rationale: honest evaluation prevents you from thinking you're performing well when you're actually peeking ahead.

Step 6: Evaluate with the right metrics. For regression, look at RMSE (root mean squared error) or MAE (mean absolute error); for classification, use accuracy, precision, recall, and F1 score. Consider a simple baseline comparison so you can see when extra complexity is helping. Rationale: metrics reveal real value and guard against overfitting or gimmicks.

Step 7: Interpret and iterate wisely. If a model barely beats the baseline, keep it simple. If a complex ensemble improves performance, check for overfitting and make sure you can explain the results in business terms. Rationale: useful models must be understandable enough to trust and act on.

Two short examples to see the steps in action

Example 1: Regression to forecast tomorrow's close. You start with past prices and volume, add a couple of moving averages, and run a simple linear regression. The baseline gives a readable error metric. If you notice improvement with a small tree-based ensemble, you test it on the validation set. If the ensemble consistently reduces error on unseen data, you keep it but monitor for overfitting and ensure the model's signals make sense in the real market context.

Example 2: Classification to predict price direction. You label each day as up or down based on the next day's close. You begin with logistic regression, then try a small random forest. You compare accuracy and a confusion matrix to see if you're catching up with the right kind of errors. If precision for "up" is low and costly, you tweak features or thresholds, or you may decide that the extra model complexity isn't worth the gain.

Clustering and dimensionality reduction for segmentation

Clustering groups similar data points without using a predetermined label. It helps you discover natural patterns, customer segments, or regime-like behaviors in markets. Dimensionality reduction reduces the number of features while preserving as much information as possible, which makes data easier to visualize and sometimes easier to model.

Step 1: Clarify the goal of clustering. Do you want to segment customers, identify unusual activity, or simplify a broad feature set for faster modeling? Rationale: a clear aim guides how you choose the algorithm and how you interpret the results.

Step 2: Prepare and standardize features. Normalize or standardize features so that differences in scale don't bias the grouping. Handle missing values sensibly; clustering works best with clean input. Rationale: standardized data makes clusters meaningful and comparable.

Step 3: Choose a clustering method. Start with a simple method like k-means if you expect round-ish groups with similar sizes. If you expect irregular clusters or outliers, consider another method such as hierarchical clustering or DBSCAN. Rationale: different methods reveal different shapes of data and avoid forcing a flat structure onto a complex reality.

Step 4: Decide how many groups. If you're using k-means, you'll pick a number K. Use practical tests like the elbow method and silhouette scores to choose a sensible K. Rationale: too few clusters miss nuance; too many clusters split what should be a single group.

Step 5: Validate and interpret. Look at cluster centers or representative samples from each group. Do the groups align with domain knowledge, like customer behavior or risk profiles? Rationale: clusters should be interpretable and practically useful.

Step 6: Dimensionality reduction for visualization or speed. Use PCA (principal components) to reduce features to a few axes to plot or to speed up downstream tasks. Other methods like t-SNE or UMAP can help visualize high-dimensional data, especially for exploratory analysis, but use them with care for real-time decisions. Rationale: reducing dimensions can reveal hidden structure and make subsequent modeling easier.

Two short examples to illustrate clustering and reduction

Example 3: Customer segmentation. You cluster transaction features (frequency, average size, time of activity) to find groups like "light, consistent buyers" and "high-spender, irregular buyers." Mapping customers into these groups helps tailor offers and risk assessments.

Example 4: Dimensionality reduction for visualization. You collect many features from a set of assets and reduce them to two principal components so you can plot each asset on a simple map. You look for groups of assets that behave similarly, which guides diversification or hedging strategies.

Choosing between supervised and unsupervised workflows

Knowing when to use supervised versus unsupervised methods saves time and reduces frustration.

Step 1: Check for labels. If you have historical outcomes or targets you want to predict, you're in supervised territory. If you don't have labels and you want to explore structure or detect unusual patterns, you're in unsupervised territory. Rationale: labels unlock prediction; unlabeled data invites discovery.

Step 2: Decide the goal. If your goal is accurate prediction or forecasting, start with supervised models. If your aim is understanding, segmentation, or anomaly discovery without a target, start with unsupervised methods. Rationale: goals shape the method.

Step 3: Consider data quality and labeling costs. Supervised learning pays off when labels are reliable and plentiful; unsupervised learning can be valuable when labeling is scarce or expensive. Rationale: evidence and resources determine practicality.

Step 4: Be prepared for hybrid approaches. Semi-supervised and self-supervised methods can use unlabeled data to improve predictive models when labeling is limited. Ensemble methods can combine supervised and unsupervised insights for better performance. Rationale: mixing approaches lets you leverage all available information.

Step 5: Plan an evaluation that matches the goal. For supervised models, use predictive metrics and calibration checks. For unsupervised work, use cluster validity, stability over runs, and how well the results support decisions. Rationale: the right tests tell you if you're truly gaining clarity.

Two practical examples to show the choice

Example 5: Fraud detection. You have many labeled fraud events and many normal transactions; you use supervised models to predict fraud labels, track performance, and update rules as fraud patterns shift. If you notice new kinds of patterns that don't fit existing labels, you can add unsupervised detectors to catch anomalies that supervised models might miss.

Example 6: Anomaly detection in trading. You lack clean labels for anomalies but want to flag unusual price moves or atypical orders. Start with unsupervised anomaly detectors; if you later obtain labels for certain events, you can add supervised components to reduce false positives and improve confirmation speed.

Exercises

1) Build a simple regression model to forecast a basic numeric target (like next-day close) using a small feature set. Do it for 15–20 minutes, then measure RMSE on a held-out set. Compare with a baseline (like a naive last-value forecast) to see if your model adds value.

2) Create a classification model to predict a price movement (up or down). Spend 20–25 minutes, evaluate accuracy and a confusion matrix, and look at which mistakes matter most for decisions you would take in trading or risk management.

3) Run a small clustering exercise on a feature set you can access (e.g., transaction features). Use

k-means with 3–4 clusters for 15–20 minutes. Check the silhouette score and review the cluster centers to describe each group in plain terms.

4) Do a quick dimensionality reduction pass. Apply PCA on a modest feature set and look at explained variance by the first two components. Spend 15 minutes noting how much information remains after reduction and consider if you'd use the reduced features for faster modeling later.

Troubleshooting and quick fixes

- Data leakage: never use future information to train your model. Ensure temporal ordering is respected in splits and feature creation. Quick fix:

create a strict training/validation/test chronology and re-check your pipeline.

- Overfitting: a model that performs well on training data but poorly on unseen data is risky. Quick fix: simplify the model, reduce features, and increase the validation size; use regularization where appropriate.

- Feature scaling issues: many models rely on consistent feature scales. Quick fix: standardize or normalize features before training, especially for distance-based methods like KNN or SVM.

- Class imbalance: when one class dominates (like few fraud cases), accuracy can be misleading. Quick fix: use resampling, adjust class weights, or choose metrics like F1 or area under the ROC curve that reflect performance on the minority class.

- Cluster validity: clusters can look good but be meaningless. Quick fix: validate with silhouette score, compare with random baselines, and check interpretability of clusters with domain knowledge.

Templates and tools you can copy

- Model selection checklist:

  - Do you have labeled data? Yes -> supervised; No -> unsupervised.

  - Is the goal prediction, segmentation, or anomaly detection? Choose accordingly.

  - Do you need interpretability or speed? Favor simpler models first.

- Is there risk of leakage or data snooping? Audit data splits and feature creation.

- Feature engineering quick-start:

    - Include price indicators (moving averages, momentum)

    - Include volume-based features

    - Include event-based signals if relevant (earnings days, policy changes)

    - Normalize features for models that need it

- Evaluation rubric:

    - For regression: RMSE/MAE, bias, variance

    - For classification: accuracy, precision, recall, F1, ROC-AUC

- For clustering: silhouette score, cluster stability, interpretability

- Mini-pipeline template:

  - Data split (train/validation/test) by time

  - Preprocessing (scaling, missing values)

  - Model training

  - Validation and metric calculation

  - Model comparison and selection

Key Takeaway: You gain practical guardrails for choosing and combining supervised and unsupervised methods to learn from financial data without losing sight of real-world constraints.

Coming up next

Subtittle: Algorithmic Trading Strategies

1) Designing momentum, mean-reversion, and market-making rules,

2) Signal generation, parameter selection, and strategy refinement,

3) Execution logic accounting for slippage and transaction costs.

Chapter 4

Algorithmic Trading Strategies

By the end of this chapter, you will know how to design momentum, mean-reversion, and market-making rules and test them in simple, practical ways.

Momentum rules

You start with a simple idea: prices tend to keep moving in the same direction for a little while. To design a momentum rule, you set up a clear path from signal to action, with a built-in sense of when to stop. Here are practical steps you can use right away.

Step 1. Pick a horizon and a baseline. Decide whether you're looking at intraday moves, daily moves, or a few days' trend. The shorter the horizon, the more you'll react to small blips; the longer the horizon, the more you ride bigger swings. Choose a baseline that helps you measure changes over that horizon. A common choice is a simple comparison to the moving average or a recent price change over N periods.

Rationale: Momentum relies on continuation. If prices have moved up for several periods, they often keep going a bit longer; if they've fallen, they may continue downward briefly. The horizon you choose acts like a filter to separate real follow-through from random noise.

Step 2. Define your entry and exit criteria. A straightforward rule is: enter a long position when the price has risen by a threshold over the last N periods; exit when the move slows or reverses. For a short entry, look for a drop below the threshold. The exit should be rule-based too: close when the momentum signal flips or when a smaller, opposite signal appears.

Rationale: Clear rules reduce hesitation and bias. They also make it easy to test whether momentum works under different market conditions.

Step 3. Add risk controls. Require a maximum loss per trade, or cap exposure by position size relative to your starting capital. Consider optional filters, like confirming volume pickup or avoiding moments of low liquidity.

Rationale: Momentum can sometimes chase false signals, especially in choppy markets. A guardrail protects you from big losses when the market suddenly reverses.

Step 4. Example in action. Imagine a stock that has risen steadily for five days. You set a rule: if the 5-day gain exceeds 2%, you buy; you sell if the price falls back by 1% from the peak. On a day when the stock jumps 2.5%, you enter. If the next day it goes up a little more, you may take partial profit or tighten the exit rule. If the stock reverses and drops 1.5% from your peak, you exit. This is a simple, repeatable pattern you can test in different stocks and timeframes.

Mean-reversion rules

Mean reversion rests on the idea that prices drift away from a fair value and then return. Designing a mean-reversion rule means choosing a target and a window that tells you when the price has wandered too far from that target.

Step 1. Choose a mean and a window. A common approach is to use a moving average as the mean and to look at how far the current price sits from that mean in standardized terms (a simple deviation or z-score). Pick a window that makes sense for your horizon—short windows for quick bounces, longer windows for broader swings.

Rationale: The mean is a magnet. Prices often bounce back toward it after moving too far, giving you opportunities to enter when the current price becomes relatively cheap or expensive.

Step 2. Establish a deviation threshold. Set a level of deviation that flags a pullback. For example, you might decide to buy when the price is 1.5 standard deviations below the moving average and sell when it is 1.0 above. You can vary thresholds by stock, liquidity, or market regime.

Rationale: Thresholds help avoid overreacting to small, random moves. They give your strategy a disciplined way to act only when a move looks statistically meaningful.

Step 3. Define entry and exit rules. A typical setup is: go long when the price dips below the mean by a chosen amount; exit when the price reverts closer to the mean or hits a profit target. For short trades, do the opposite.

Rationale: Simple entry and exit rules keep your strategy easy to test and adjust. Clear rules also help you spot when the market isn't behaving in a mean-reverting way.

Step 4. Inventory and risk checks. In mean-reversion, you often face margin and timing risks if the market stays trending. Add a cap on how long you stay in a position, and consider a правило that reduces position size after a few adverse moves.

Rationale: Markets can stay trending longer than you expect. A break-even or small-loss exit prevents a temporary trend from turning into a blown account.

Step 5. Example in action. Suppose the moving average over 20 periods is your reference, and you observe that the price has fallen 2 standard deviations below that average. You enter a long position, expecting a return toward the mean. If the price climbs back toward the mean within a few days, you exit with a small gain. If the price continues to fall, your risk controls help you cut losses early rather than letting a larger decline unfold.

Market-making rules

Market making focuses on providing liquidity and earning the difference between bid and ask prices. This approach requires careful quoting, inventory awareness, and fast adjustments to changing conditions.

Step 1. Set an initial mid-price and spread. The mid-price is the average of the best bid and best ask. Your spread is the distance you quote around that mid-price. A tight spread helps trades happen, but you must manage the risk of frequent inventory moves.

Rationale: Market making relies on capturing small, frequent profits from many trades. A predictable spread helps counterparties know where you stand and keeps activity flowing.

Step 2. Update quotes with the market. Adjust quotes based on price movement, volatility, and your current inventory. If you own a lot of stock, you might widen the spread or be willing to buy back more conservatively to reduce risk.

Rationale: Flexible quotes protect you from sudden price swings and help you avoid holding too much of one asset when the market shifts.

Step 3. Manage inventory risk. Set limits for how much you can accumulate of a single asset and how quickly you will unwind if prices move unfavorably. Use a stopping rule to reduce exposure when the position grows too large.

Rationale: Inventory risk is real. Even if you earn the spread most days, a big adverse move can erase profits quickly.

Step 4. Execution discipline. Decide how you will fill orders when the market moves. Do you chase a better price, or do you wait for a fair price to come back? Pick a method that balances speed, cost, and risk.

Rationale: Execution discipline prevents wild swings in results caused by impatient or impulsive actions.

Step 5. Example in action. Consider a market with a tight, steady spread. You quote slightly tighter than the average, and you adjust as the stock moves and as your inventory changes. If you notice you're accumulating too much of the stock, you widen the spread and reduce new buys to prevent a larger drift. If liquidity dries up, you gracefully reduce activity to protect capital while staying engaged for future opportunities.

Section 2: Signal generation, parameter selection, and strategy refinement

This section explains how you turn the ideas above into practical signals you can test, tune, and improve over time.

Step 1. Generate signals from simple rules. Use easy-to-follow indicators like price changes over a short window, how far the price sits from a moving average, or the relationship between price and volume. The goal is to produce clear, repeatable signals with minimal ambiguity.

Rationale: Clear signals are easy to test across stocks and markets. Simple rules let you understand why a trade happened and how it might be improved.

Step 2. Pick parameters with care. Choose windows, thresholds, and lookback periods that reflect the asset's liquidity and typical price movements. Start with conservative values and expand gradually. Avoid chasing a single favorable outcome that you found in one stock or one period.

Rationale: Parameters shape how your signals behave. Small changes can lead to big differences in performance, especially in noisy markets.

Step 3. Refine strategies across regimes. Test your rules in different market environments: rising, falling, and sideways. If a rule only works in a single regime, adapt it or pair it with another rule that covers other conditions.

Rationale: Markets are not uniform. A robust strategy performs reasonably well in many situations, not just in one.

Step 4. Example in action. You test a momentum rule using a 5-day horizon and a 2% threshold on several stocks across a month that included a rally and a small pullback. You observe that some stocks perform better in strong uptrends, while others drift in choppier periods. You add a simple check: if volume doesn't rise with price, you defer entry. The refined rule reduces trades in weak volume days and keeps you in play when momentum is real.

Step 5. A broader look at signals. For mean-reversion, you test a threshold that is too tight and you notice frequent false entries. You loosen the threshold slightly and add a short cooldown window after each exit to avoid rapid re-entries. For market-making, you test different spreads and inventory caps. You find a sweet spot where profit per trade stays steady while the number of trades remains manageable.

Step 6. How to monitor progress. Track how often signals fire, the average holding period, and the average gain or loss per trade. If you see too many tiny wins that don't cover costs, you adjust by widening the criteria or reducing the number of entries.

Rationale: Ongoing tuning helps you keep your rules useful as markets evolve. It also helps you separate real skill from luck.

Section 3: Execution logic accounting for slippage and transaction costs

The last major block of practical design is how you actually place and fill orders. Slippage and costs matter a lot for any short-term trading approach.

Step 1. Understand slippage and how it happens. Slippage is the difference between the expected fill price and the price you actually get. It happens when the market moves, when there isn't enough liquidity, or when your order size is large relative to the market.

Rationale: Slippage eats into profits, especially in fast markets. Recognize it early so you can plan around it rather than chase perfect fills.

Step 2. Choose order types and venues wisely. Use order types that fit your goal, such as limit orders when you want price control and market orders when speed matters. Consider the liquidity of the venue and the typical costs charged there. If possible, break large orders into smaller pieces to reduce market impact.

Rationale: The right mix of order types helps you balance price certainty with fill probability and cost.

Step 3. Plan order slicing and pacing. For larger orders, split into smaller chunks and space them out over time or across different moments of day.

Use rules like “fill a portion at a time” and “pause if price moves beyond a threshold.” This reduces the chance of a big price jump against you.

Rationale: Slicing smooths execution and lowers the risk of a single, costly fill.

Step 4. Account for transaction costs. Include commissions, exchange fees, and any other charges in your profitability math. If costs are high, you may need tighter spreads, quicker exits, or more selective entry criteria to stay profitable.

Rationale: Costs are real, and they change the bottom line just as much as price moves do.

Step 5. Realistic risk controls during execution. Set guardrails like a maximum daily loss, a cap on the number of trades per day, or an overall limit on the amount of capital exposed at any moment. If a day looks too choppy or costs spike, slow down or pause activity.

Rationale: Raw speed without discipline often leads to bigger losses than you expect.

Step 6. Examples in action. Example A: A momentum entry that relies on a rapid price rise is accompanied by a timed exit if the move fades within a set window. You use a limit order to enter, and a smaller profit target to cap risk. If liquidity drops, you cancel or delay the order to avoid a bad fill. Example B: A market-making scenario on a stock with a narrow spread. You place small, frequent quotes and adjust your spread when you notice a shift in inventory. If the stock becomes unusually volatile, you reduce exposure and widen quotes to protect capital.

Step 7. Quick checks and pitfalls. A common pitfall is assuming back-tested performance transfers to live trading without error. Markets change, data quality matters, and slippage can erase edge. Always sanity-check your assumptions with a test run in a simulated environment before risking real capital. Another pitfall is ignoring data latency. If your data feed arrives late, your signals reflect yesterday's prices, not today's reality. Address this by using timely data streams and validating your pipeline end-to-end.

Key Takeaway: Simple, repeatable rules with clear signals and disciplined execution beat flashy, hard-to-test ideas. Coming up next: Backtesting and Performance Evaluation

1) Building realistic backtest engines and proper data splits

2) Performance metrics: returns, Sharpe, drawdowns, and turnover

3) Techniques to detect and prevent overfitting and look-ahead bias

Transition: In the next chapter, you'll learn how to build a practical backtest engine, split data wisely to test your strategies fairly, and read performance metrics without chasing short-term luck. You'll also explore ways to spot overfitting and avoid look-ahead biases so your results stay trustworthy across markets.

Chapter 5

Backtesting and Performance Evaluation

By the end of this chapter you will be able to run backtests that resemble real trading, read the performance metrics clearly, and spot signs of overfitting.

Backtesting Engines and Data Splits

You build a backtest engine to pretend you are trading in the past, using only information that would have been available at the time. The goal is to measure how a rule would have behaved in a real environment, not to "tune" the past to look perfect. Start by setting the scope: choose a market or set of securities, a time period, and the rule you will test. Then gather data that is clean and consistent across the entire period you will evaluate.

Step 1: Define the universe and time frame. Decide which assets you will trade and the window you will study. A tighter universe makes it easier to understand results; a broader one tests robustness. The key is to stay consistent in how you apply the rule across the entire window.

Step 2: Verify data quality and integrity. Check that prices align with dates, that missing values are handled in a transparent way, and that corporate actions are accounted for. If you find gaps, decide on a respectful approach and stick to it. Consistency matters more than chasing perfect data.

Step 3: Create a chronological data split. Do not mix future data into your calibration. Split the historical record into a calibration period (for building or tuning the rule) and a subsequent evaluation period (to see how the rule would perform in unseen data). This forward-looking split helps prevent bias that looks good on paper but would fail in real trading.

Step 4: Build the execution model. Simulate fills, slippage, and commissions as they would occur in real life. If you can, include a basic market impact model so heavy trades don't appear magically cost-free. Record the assumptions you use about slippage and costs so you can review them later.

Step 5: Run the backtest and run quick sanity checks. Look for obvious issues like trades happening before the rule is activated or a sudden jump in results that doesn't match market behavior. Compare the engine's output with a simple baseline, such as a buy-and-hold strategy on the same data, to see if the results feel plausible.

Step 6: Document and align. Keep notes on the data sources, split dates, rule parameters, and cost assumptions. A clear audit trail helps you explain results and prevents accidental bias during later reviews.

Examples

Example 1: Moving-average crossover. You test a rule that buys when a shorter moving average crosses above a longer one and sells when it crosses below. You choose a 50-day and a 200-day average for daily data over two years. Calibration uses the first 18 months; evaluation uses the last 6 months. You include a modest per-trade slippage and a small commission per round trip. When you finish, you compare the strategy to a buy-and-hold baseline on the same two-year window and note how often the rule would have traded and what the overall return looks like. The backtest shows how sensitive results are to the split date and to costs, which helps you decide whether to trust the signal.

Example 2: Momentum with walk-forward testing. You test a momentum rule that buys assets with rising prices and sells those with falling prices. You break the data into several consecutive blocks: calibrate on block one, evaluate on block two, then roll forward to block three and repeat. This walk-forward approach mimics how you would adjust a live system over time, without peeking into the future. You record each block's performance and look for stability across blocks. If one block dramatically outperforms the others, you investigate to see whether the result is due to luck or to a genuine signal.

Performance Metrics

You measure success with metrics that tell you not just how much you earned, but how reliably and at what cost. The four core metrics you should know are returns, the Sharpe ratio, drawdowns, and turnover. Each one answers a different question about your strategy's behavior.

Returns

Return is the total gain from the start to the end of the evaluation period, often expressed as a percentage. You can also look at annualized return to compare across periods. A higher return is good, but not by itself. You must see how much risk was taken to achieve that return.

Example: If your portfolio grows from 100 to 120 over a year, the simple return is 20%. If you held for two years and grew from 100 to 140, the annualized return would be about 9.5% per year, assuming smooth growth. Real-life results vary with market conditions and the costs of trading.

Sharpe Ratio

The Sharpe ratio measures risk-adjusted return. It asks: how much extra return did you earn for each unit of risk you took? The basic idea is to subtract a risk-free rate (what you could earn with a safe investment) from your return, then divide by how volatile your returns were. A higher Sharpe means you earned more per unit of risk.

Formula in plain terms: Sharpe roughly equals (average return minus risk-free return) divided by the standard deviation of returns. In practice you can use convenient approximations, especially in teaching settings, but remember that higher Sharpe generally signals better risk-adjusted performance.

Example: If your annual return is 15% and the risk-free rate is 2%, and your portfolio's standard deviation is 10%, the Sharpe ratio is about (0.15 - 0.02) / 0.10 = 1.3. This number helps you compare with other strategies or with the market.

Drawdowns

Drawdown is the decline from a peak value to a trough before the next peak. It shows how bad a period of losses can be, which helps you understand the worst-case pain a strategy could experience. You track the largest peak-to-trough drop and how long it lasts. A strategy with shallow drawdowns and quick recoveries is generally easier to tolerate and manage.

Example: If your portfolio grows to a high of 100 and then falls to 92 before rising again, the drawdown is 8%. If the dip lasts several months, you consider the time horizon you can tolerate and what would be reasonable to expect in turbulent markets.

Turnover

Turnover measures how often you trade. Higher turnover means more transaction costs and more exposure to short-term risk. Lower turnover often means a smoother ride and fewer costs, but it can also mean missing opportunities. The key is to understand how much activity your rules generate and what that means for costs and tax considerations.

Example: Turnover of 60% in a year means, on average, more than half your holdings were traded within the year. If costs are high, that turnover can erode returns even when the gross performance looks good.

Techniques to Detect and Prevent Overfitting and Look-Ahead Bias

Overfitting happens when a rule is tailored so tightly to historical quirks that it loses usefulness in new data. Look-ahead bias occurs when information from the future leaks into the past, producing untrustworthy results. You guard against both with several practical practices.

Step 1: Use clear out-of-sample testing. Calibrate rules on one portion of the data, then evaluate on a separate, unseen portion. Treat that second portion as if it were live trading. If the rule fails in the out-of-sample period, you probably overfitted or relied on a data quirk.

Step 2: Apply walk-forward analysis. Break the data into multiple sequential blocks. Calibrate on one block, test on the next, then roll forward. This approach shows how the rule performs across different market regimes and reduces the chance that a single favorable period drives the results.

Step 3: Predefine parameter ranges and limits. Do not search for a single perfect set of parameters after you see the results. Decide in advance which parameter values you will test, and stick to that plan. This discipline reduces data snooping and bias.

Step 4: Favor simplicity and robustness. Complex rules can capture noise better than signal. Start with simple rules and add complexity only if it clearly improves robust performance across multiple markets and time periods.

Step 5: Use regularization and conservative assumptions. If you use many inputs or features, apply methods that prevent any one input from dominating the decision. Keep cost assumptions reasonable and consistent across tests to avoid artificial advantages.

Step 6: Guard against data leakage. Double-check that your splits truly separate the data in time, that features derived in calibration period aren't engineered using information from the evaluation period, and that you don't reuse the same data to both calibrate and evaluate.

Examples

Example 1: Out-of-sample test reveals a quirk. You calibrate a rule on the first two years of data and test on the third year. The rule performs well in calibration but poorly in the third year. Investigating, you find a market event in the first year that didn't recur. You adjust by tightening the rule or using a filter that reduces signals during unusual events. The outcome is a more robust approach that avoids overreacting to a single episode.

Example 2: Walk-forward detects regime change. You run a walk-forward test across four blocks. The rule shines in blocks 1 and 2 but underperforms in blocks 3 and 4, which correspond to a different market regime. You respond by adding a simple regime-detection component or by limiting parameter changes between blocks. The result is a strategy that adapts more gracefully rather than chasing a moving target.

Exercises

Exercise 1. Data split practice. Take a short data set of daily prices for a year. Split it into calibration and evaluation periods. Run a simple rule in calibration, then test it in evaluation. Write down the performance difference and note what changed when you moved to evaluation. Time: 20 minutes. Outcome: you can reproduce a clean out-of-sample test and recognize when results fail in unseen data.

Exercise 2. Cost and slippage estimation. Add a modest per-trade cost and a simple slippage model to your backtest. Run a baseline strategy with and without the costs. Compare the results and explain how costs affect turnover and net return. Time: 15 minutes. Outcome: you understand how costs erode performance and how to reflect them honestly.

Exercise 3. Walk-forward setup. Create four consecutive blocks of data. Calibrate a rule on block 1, test on block 2, calibrate on block 3, test on block 4. Record performance in each block and look for consistency. Time: 30 minutes. Outcome: you can implement walk-forward testing and observe regime sensitivity.

Optional Exercise 4. Simple sensitivity check. Change one parameter within a reasonable range and observe how performance changes in the evaluation period. Do not search for the best value; just note whether small changes make the results much worse or only slightly different. Time: 15 minutes. Outcome: you see how stable your results are to parameter shifts.

Troubleshooting

Problem: The backtest shows perfect profits with no drawdown. Fix: Check for data leakage and ensure the evaluation period is truly out-of-sample.

Re-run with a clean split and a simple baseline to compare.

Problem: A sudden jump in performance after a long flat period. Fix: Look for a data artifact, such as a missing price or a normalization error. Validate data handling steps and test again with a transparent workflow.

Problem: Turnover is unexpectedly high. Fix: Review signal generation and costs. Consider adding a filter to reduce trades during noisy periods or using a rule that requires stronger confirmation before trading.

Tools and Templates

Backtest Setup Checklist

Define the universe and time horizon clearly.

Check data quality and actionability for the entire window.

Choose a chronological data split and document dates.

Specify cost assumptions: commissions, slippage, and market impact.

Build a transparent execution model and record your assumptions.

Run calibration and evaluation, then review results with a simple baseline.

Data Split Template

Calibration period: start date to split date

Evaluation period: split date to end date

Rules: list the trading rule parameters

Costs: per-trade estimates, spreads, and round-trip commissions

Key Takeaway: Realistic backtests depend on clean data splits, careful cost modeling, and honest checks that guard against bias and overfitting.

Coming up next: Risk Management and Portfolio Construction

In the next chapter, you will learn how to size positions, diversify wisely, and control leverage, plus how to stress test scenarios and apply value-at-risk concepts. You will also see how AI signals can influence allocation and rebalancing rules, preparing you for safer, smarter decisions across a wider portfolio.

Chapter 6

Risk Management and Portfolio Construction

By the end of this chapter, you will know how to size positions, diversify, and use AI signals to guide allocation and rebalancing in a safe, repeatable way.

1) Position sizing, diversification, and leverage controls

Your first job is to size each bet in a way that the whole portfolio stays steady even when some bets go against you. Position sizing is the practice of deciding how big a single investment should be relative to your total capital. Diversification means spreading bets across different assets, sectors, or strategies so that a single bad outcome doesn't wipe you out. Leverage controls are guardrails that limit how much you borrow to amplify bets, so you don't overextend your capital.

Do this in three practical steps. Step one is to define your total capital and how much risk you're willing to accept per position. A common, simple rule is to risk a small portion of your portfolio on any one trade or bet—enough that a few losses won't derail your plans, but not so small that you miss important opportunities. For many beginners, risking about 1% to 2% of total capital per position is a reasonable starting point. If you have $100,000 saved, that means a single bet should be able to lose about $1,000 to $2,000 without breaking your bank. The exact numbers depend on your comfort with risk and your timeline, but aim for a plan you can defend when markets get choppier.

Step two is to build diversification into the core of your portfolio. Diversification is more than owning many things; it's about owning things that don't all move the same way at the same time. Think of assets that have different kinds of risk and different drivers. Add some variety across asset classes, time horizons, and investment styles. The goal is that when one asset slides, others may hold steady or rise, helping you avoid big swings in overall value. A practical target is to include enough independent bets so that the portfolio's performance isn't dominated by a single factor or event. Diversification also means avoiding over-reliance on any single AI signal or model unless you explicitly assign it a smaller share of your portfolio.

Step three is to set clear leverage controls. Leverage can magnify gains, but it can also magnify losses and shorten the time you have to recover. Put a cap on how much you borrow to fund positions and cap the total exposure you take on any given day or week. If a position could push your drawdown beyond your comfort zone, you should either reduce its size or remove it. In practice, this means you maintain a practical margin or collateral plan, set a hard limit on aggregated leverage, and review it regularly as your capital grows or your risk appetite changes. The aim is discipline, not bravado.

Two quick micro-cases help anchor this. Case one: you hold five different bets, each with a risk cap of 1% of your capital. If two bets move badly at the same time, their combined risk still remains contained because you capped each position and kept track of how many bets you carry at once. Case two: you're tempted to add a high-volatility asset because your AI signals look exciting. Before you push the button, check how much extra diversification you'd gain and whether the new bet would push your total leverage past your limit. If it does, scale back somewhere else first.

A practical rule of thumb is to think in terms of risk contribution rather than raw dollar size. This means asking not only how big a position is, but how much risk it adds to the entire portfolio. If one position could contribute more than its share to downside, trim it back. If a sector move creates lower risk than you expected, you may be able to increase exposure slightly—but only within your overall risk budget.

A simple template you can use starts with three lines: Total capital, Risk per position, and Maximum number of active positions. Then, for each new idea, compute position size from risk per position and the cushion you want against worst-case price moves. Make a quick note of the maximum allowed leverage after adding the new bet. If the math doesn't balance with your rules, skip or adjust until it does.

Examples show the idea in action. Example one: you have $100,000. You decide to risk $1,000 per position. Suppose you're considering a trade with a stop loss that implies a $50 move per unit. The maximum number of units you should buy is 1,000 divided by 50, which is 20 units. If you plan to hold five such bets, you are at a total potential risk of $5,000 if every stop is hit, which is 5% of your capital—an amount you've determined you're comfortable absorbing in rough markets. Example two: you want to diversify across stocks, bonds, and a small slice of an alternative asset. You run the numbers to ensure no single bet can push your portfolio into a level you can't recover from, given your leverage cap. If one new idea would push you past that cap, you either reduce the size of another bet or skip the idea for now.

Key to all this is staying transparent about your rules. Write them down in a short checklist: how you determine risk per position, how you decide the number of simultaneous bets, what your maximum leverage is, and how you adjust when markets get tougher. The calmer you are about these rules, the more you'll resist exciting but risky impulses.

2) Stress testing, scenario analysis, and value-at-risk methods

Stress testing and scenario analysis are about looking ahead to tough times and asking, "What would happen to my portfolio if this happened?" They're not predictions; they're risk checks that help you see potential weaknesses before they bite. Value-at-risk, or VaR, is a statistical idea that tries to answer a simple question: how much could I lose in a bad day, a bad week, or a bad month with a given level of confidence? The essence is not to chase perfect precision but to create a guardrail that helps you stay within your risk tolerance when reality proves harsher than your best-case assumptions.

Start with a practical three-step process. Step one is to define a couple of concrete scenarios that feel plausible given current conditions. Think in terms of market-wide pullbacks (for example, broad equity declines), regime shifts (like a sudden rise in volatility or a shift in interest rates), and sector-specific shocks (such as a technology downturn). You don't need grand prognostications; you need reasonable, possible outcomes to test against. Step two is to apply those scenarios to your existing portfolio and measure the losses. This means revaluing your positions as if the scenario had occurred and summing the result. The goal isn't to predict the exact loss you'll see but to understand whether your risk controls—your diversification, your risk per position, and any hedges you hold—still keep losses within your tolerance.

Step three is to use VaR as a planning tool rather than a precise forecast. VaR gives you a number that represents a worst-case loss over a chosen horizon at a given confidence level. It's a single, digestible number that can guide decision-making, but it has limitations. It does not capture every kind of risk, especially tail events that happen rarely but hurt badly, and it assumes some market behavior stays consistent. Use VaR alongside stress tests and scenario analysis to build a more complete picture of potential downsides, then translate that picture into action. If your stress tests reveal that multiple scenarios could push you past your loss tolerance, you should consider hedges, additional diversification, or reducing exposure.

Two short micro-cases illustrate the idea. Case one: during a simulated market downturn, your stock bets and your tech-focused AI signals both lose value. You see that your diversified bonds and low-correlation assets help cushion the blow, which confirms you're not overly concentrated in riskier bets. You decide to keep your diversification intact but add a modest hedge that protects against the downside in equities. Case two: a shock scenario where volatility spikes. VaR shows a higher potential loss than you're comfortable with, so you tighten some positions a touch, boost cash reserves, and adjust stop levels to reduce the chance of large, rapid losses.

A straightforward, practical approach to implementing these tools is to build a small, repeatable process. Step one: list 3 to 5 scenarios you want to test. Step two: for each scenario, run a quick valuation of every asset in your portfolio and sum the results. Step three: note the total loss and compare it to your risk budget. If you're over budget, adjust until you're within it, either by trimming positions, changing hedges, or rebalancing to a safer mix. A simple "Scenario Sheet" can help: Scenario name, Description, Expected loss, Action if loss exceeds limit. This sheet becomes a living document you update as market conditions change.

Two concrete examples reinforce the habit. Example one: you test a 15% equity market drop plus a 5% rise in volatility. You find that while some growth bets lose more than you'd like, your bond and cash-like assets hold up better, and your overall loss stays within your plan. You decide to maintain the mix but add a modest hedging position to protect the downside further. Example two: you test a rate shock that would push longer-term bonds down in price. If your AI signals point toward credit risk increasing under that shock, you adjust by reducing duration exposure and shifting toward shorter-duration assets, staying within your risk framework.

In practice, many beginners find it helpful to couple simple, repeatable tests with a public-facing, internal risk dashboard. The dashboard can show at a glance the current portfolio exposure, the worst-case losses under your chosen scenarios, and the status of each hedge you hold. You don't need elaborate software to start; a basic spreadsheet with a few clearly labeled columns can do the job. The rule of thumb is to keep your risk checks as regular as your daily routine, not something you only do occasionally when markets feel scary.

3) Incorporating AI signals into allocation and rebalancing rules

Artificial intelligence can offer valuable signals about how assets might move, but the real power comes when you translate those signals into disciplined allocation and rebalancing rules rather than letting them drive reflexive bets. The core idea is to use AI as a guide that informs weights, while still respecting your established risk limits and diversification goals. This means you map AI scores to weights, set guardrails, and keep a steady cadence for rebalancing.

Start with a practical three-step approach. Step one is to map AI signals to allocation weights with guardrails. For each asset or asset class, assign a base weight that reflects your long-term plan. Then adjust those weights based on AI scores, but constrain the adjustments with minimum and maximum bounds. A simple guardrail can be something like: no single asset can exceed a maximum weight, and a minimum baseline keeps you from starving a diversification idea. Step two is to set a disciplined rebalancing cadence. Decide how often you'll rebalance—monthly, quarterly, or after a set threshold change in AI signals. The cadence should be regular enough to capture meaningful changes, but not so frequent that transaction costs erode returns. Step three is to test the AI-informed rules with backtests and "paper" runs before you apply them to real capital. Backtests help you see how the rules would have behaved in the past, while paper runs show how you'd act in real time without risking capital.

Two micro-cases illustrate the approach. Case one: your AI system rates technology stocks as high potential today. You increase your base weight for tech, but you cap it so tech can't dominate the portfolio. If the AI signal weakens in the next window, you trim tech back toward the cap, preserving diversification while staying responsive to the signal. Case two: a multi-asset AI model signals a regime shift toward higher volatility. You raise cash in a controlled way, reallocate some weights toward less volatile assets, and tighten stop levels to keep downside risk manageable. The key is to keep AI signals as a guide, not a dictator, and to preserve core risk controls.

A practical template helps operationalize this approach. An AI-informed allocation rule might look like this: start with baseline weights that reflect your plan; adjust each weight up or down based on scaled AI scores; apply max and min bounds to each asset; rebalance on your chosen cadence; monitor the total portfolio risk after each adjustment. Pair this with a simple "risk guard" checklist that asks: did any single asset exceed its max weight? did overall risk rise beyond your target? If yes, adjust before placing new trades.

Two additional notes help keep AI signals reliable. First, avoid overfitting by testing your rules on past data and across different market regimes. If a rule only worked in a narrow period, it might not survive future conditions. Second, combine AI signals with human judgment and traditional risk metrics. AI can reveal patterns the eye misses, but risk controls, diversification, and clear decision boundaries should always govern how you act.

Key Takeaway: Use AI signals to inform allocations, but lock them inside a disciplined framework of risk limits, diversification, and tested rebalancing rules.

Coming up next: Fraud Detection and Anomaly Identification will discuss pattern recognition for payments fraud and anti-money laundering, real-time scoring and case management, and hybrid systems that blend rules, supervised models, and unsupervised detectors.

Chapter 7

Fraud Detection and Anomaly Identification

By the end of this chapter you will know how to recognize fraud patterns, set up real-time scoring and alert triage, and build hybrid detection systems that combine rules with models.

Pattern recognition for payments fraud and anti-money laundering

You start by looking for patterns. Patterns are telltale shapes in data that tell you something isn't quite right. In payments, patterns show up as unusual sequences: many small payments in a short period, new devices or locations appearing for a customer, or a sudden cluster of transfers moving toward destinations that don't fit a customer's normal history. In anti-money laundering work, patterns may be rapid transfers across multiple accounts, bursts of activity tied to a single customer, or funds moving through accounts that share similar timing but don't have obvious legitimate reasons. You don't need to memorize every possible trick to start spotting red flags; you just need a practical way to notice when something looks off.

Data you'll rely on includes transaction records (who paid whom, when, how much), customer profiles (how a person normally acts, preferred payment methods, typical geography), device and network signals (where the customer is logging in from, what device they use), and relationships between accounts (are accounts frequently exchanging funds, sharing phone numbers, or devices). With this mix, you can spot deviations and, over time, learn which signals tend to precede fraud versus those that are harmless quirks.

Think of your approach in three parts. First, rules that codify well-known fraud patterns. For example, a rule might flag when a single account makes a burst of payments to many new recipients within a short timeframe, or when a customer logs in from a new country and immediately initiates risky transfers. Second, unsupervised anomaly detection. This looks for data points that don't fit the normal pattern without needing labeled examples. If an event sits far from the usual cluster of legitimate activity, it deserves a closer look. Third, supervised modeling. If you have labeled examples—transactions that were fraud or legitimate—you can train a model to weigh signals and predict risk. The model doesn't replace the rules or the anomaly detectors; it adds a probabilistic judgment that helps you decide what to do next.

Two micro-cases illustrate how patterns come to life. In the first case, a retailer's payments network notices many small card-not-present transactions showing up from a few new devices within a single day. The pattern isn't obvious from one signal alone, but the combination of new devices, rapid payments, and unusual purchase categories raises a flag. A rule-based check confirms the pattern, an unsupervised detector highlights this event as an outlier, and a supervised model assigns a higher risk score because similar patterns previously led to fraud. In the second case, a bank sees a customer who suddenly transfers funds to several unfamiliar destinations in a compact time window. The activity looks suspicious when considered as a whole, even if any single transfer seems ordinary in isolation. The system lumps these events into a pattern cluster associated with AML risk, and the activity is queued for human review or automatic containment depending on your policy.

As you work with patterns, you'll also learn when to be patient. Some patterns appear only after you accumulate more data or observe a wider context. In those cases, you keep the signal and watch for corroborating evidence from other signals—geography, device changes, or recurring timing in a customer's activity—before taking stronger action. Your goal is not to block every suspicious event, but to distinguish the truly risky ones from routine activity with clear, explainable reasoning.

Real-time scoring, alert prioritization, and case management

Real-time scoring is your frontline defense. For each event—every payment, login, or transfer—you compute a risk score that reflects how likely it is to be fraud or AML. A high score triggers immediate actions, such as blocking a payment, requiring extra verification, or routing the case to a fraud analyst. A mid-range score might lead to enhanced monitoring, while a low score lets a transaction continue with normal processing. The key is to apply scores quickly and consistently, so you don't waste time on obvious risk while you miss subtle but dangerous activity.

Alert prioritization turns scores into practical work. Not all alerts deserve the same attention. You rank alerts by a combination of the risk score, the potential impact, and the context around the event (for example, a high-risk transfer from a known high-risk geography carries more weight than a similar transfer from a typical customer). You then triage the top alerts first, using a simple decision framework: verify quickly, escalate to a human reviewer if needed, or auto-flag for blocking if confidence is high. This helps you avoid alert fatigue, where analysts become numb to constant warnings and miss the real threats.

Case management is how you organize investigations. When an alert is serious, you don't treat it as a single, isolated event. You group related events into a case: multiple transactions from the same customer, related devices, or linked accounts. In the case file you record what happened, what signals contributed, what actions you took, and what the next steps are. Case management makes it possible for a team to collaborate: one person flags a case, another adds notes, and a supervisor approves the final decision. Proper case management preserves an audit trail and helps you learn from each investigation so patterns and rules improve over time.

Two practical scenes show how this works in real life. Scene one: an online retailer processes a wave of payments that look normal in isolation but share a device fingerprint and a nearby location. The real-time scoring engine assigns a moderate-high risk because the combination of device anomaly and location shift aligns with known fraud patterns. The alert is prioritized, opened as a case, and queued for a quick review. The reviewer confirms the pattern fits a known scam, and the system temporarily blocks the payments while requesting additional verification from the customer. Scene two: a corporate customer initiates several cross-border transfers to a high-risk country. The scoring model raises risk due to the amount, the counterparties, and the transfer pace. The alert is escalated to AML specialists, and the case is enriched with contextual data like related accounts and historical behavior, guiding a careful, compliant investigation rather than a blunt block.

Operationally, you design the alerts to be actionable. Each alert should carry enough context to explain why it was raised and what the recommended next step is. You tie actions to policy: if a score crosses a threshold, automatic steps—like requiring 2FA or suspending a transfer—kick in. If the score sits in a gray zone, the case is assigned to a human analyst for review, complete with links to relevant data, prior investigations, and a suggested line of questioning. You also build in feedback loops: analysts annotate outcomes, the system learns from corrections, and risk scores adjust over time to reduce false positives without letting real threats slip through.

A few practical patterns help you refine real-time scoring and triage. Use context: a customer's history, typical channels, and preferred payment methods matter as much as raw numbers. Use correlation: an alert is more trustworthy when several signals point in the same direction (for example, unusual login plus a sudden change in payment behavior). Use containment: when risk is clearly high, you should not rely on a single measure; you implement layered checks (verification, temporary holds, and cautious release as appropriate). Finally, balance speed with accuracy. Fraud prevention works best when it moves fast enough to stop bad activity but slowly enough to avoid disrupting legitimate customers.

Hybrid systems combining rules, supervised models, and unsupervised detectors

This is the core of a resilient defense. You keep three complementary engines running side by side and allow them to inform each other. The rules encode what you know works already: clear-cut fraud signals, policy violations, or compliance red flags. They're fast and transparent because you can explain exactly why each rule fired. Supervised models bring learning from historical data. They weigh the importance of many signals at once, can adapt as patterns shift, and provide probability-based risk scores you can trust for nuanced decisions. Unsupervised detectors search for new, unseen patterns without labeled data. They catch novel tricks that you haven't explicitly coded yet and can spotlight clusters or anomalies that don't fit existing rules or model patterns.

Bringing these together is not a clash; it's a fusion. You fuse their outputs into a final risk assessment. A simple approach is to combine scores or flags into a single decision variable, then apply policy thresholds to decide whether to block, challenge, monitor, or pass. A more nuanced approach uses a weighted ensemble where each component contributes to the final action with its own level of confidence. Whatever method you choose, keep it transparent. Document how each signal contributes to the final decision, so audits and reviews are straightforward.

Two micro-cases illustrate the power of hybrid systems. Case A shows a pattern that rules alone would catch, but a missing signal could have led to a false negative. A known fraud pattern fires a rule because transferring amounts and destinations match a common scam script. A supervised model also flags high risk due to historical cues. An unsupervised detector confirms there's an unusual network of accounts linked by timing and device usage, reinforcing the decision to hold the payment and investigate. Case B demonstrates a new, clever fraud that rules don't anticipate yet. A cluster of small, rapid transfers appears from multiple accounts with a shared device. The unsupervised detector spots the pattern as a new anomaly; the supervised model—trained on past examples—gives a moderate risk, and the rules don't fire yet. The hybrid system still flags the event with enough confidence to bring human investigators into the loop before any money moves, preserving safety while you learn the new trick.

As you implement a hybrid system, you should keep a few guardrails in place. First, maintain a clear data lineage so you can explain why a decision was made. Second, monitor drift: signals that used to predict fraud well can change over time; you'll need to retrain models and update rules. Third, guard against alert fatigue by tuning thresholds and grouping related alerts into tight, meaningful cases. Fourth, respect privacy and regulatory requirements. Your system should be auditable, compliant, and designed to protect customer rights even as you guard against misuse.

Troubleshooting and practical tips

Common problems pop up when you bring these tools to life. You might see too many false positives, waking you up at night with nuisance alerts. If that happens, revisit the feature set and rules, confirm data quality, and lower thresholds selectively for low-impact channels. Latency can plague real-time scoring. If decisions lag, reduce feature complexity for speed, or isolate the most time-sensitive signals for immediate scoring. Data gaps break patterns you rely on. Create defaults or fallback paths for missing information and document how you handle gaps. Model drift can erode accuracy. Schedule regular reviews, refresh data, and adjust thresholds as patterns evolve. Finally, beware of overfitting in supervised models. Use simple cross-validation, watch out for leakage, and test on fresh data that mirrors real-time conditions.

Tools, templates, and quick-start aids

Use simple, reusable artifacts to keep your process practical. A Fraud Pattern Checklist helps you track known signals and their rules. A Real-Time Scoring Template captures the signals you evaluate, the risk score, and the action taken. A Hybrid System Diagram shows how rules, models, and detectors feed into the final decision. An Alert Triage Worksheet records the priority, recommended next steps, and status so you can track outcomes and improve over time. These templates aren't about clever jargon; they're about consistency, transparency, and learning.

Exercises

Exercise 1: Map a known fraud pattern in a dataset you have access to. Identify at least three signals (one from transactions, one from behavior, one from device or network data). Write down the rule you would use, the anomaly detector signal you'd trust, and how a supervised model would help. Time for completion: 20 minutes. Expected outcome: a draft pattern map you can test against real data.

Exercise 2: Simulate 12 real-time events. Score each event, assign an alert priority, and decide whether to block, verify, or monitor. Record your decisions and the outcomes, then review which signals mattered most. Time: 15 minutes. Expected outcome: a small decision log you can compare with future results.

Exercise 3: Design a tiny hybrid decision flow. List one rule, one supervised cue, and one unsupervised detector you would combine. Describe how you would fuse their outputs and what policy would trigger an automatic hold versus a human review. Time: 25 minutes. Expected outcome: a practical fusion plan you can prototype.

Exercise 4: Review a past case or simulated case and write down three lessons learned. Note what signals were decisive, what you would adjust in rules, and how you would tune the model or detector to avoid similar gaps in the future. Time: 20 minutes. Expected outcome: a lessons-and-improvements note for ongoing iteration.

Key Takeaway: A layered approach that combines clear rules, learning from past data, and discovery of new patterns gives you a stronger, faster, and more adaptable shield against fraud and money-laundering threats.

Coming up next Subtittle: Time-Series Forecasting Techniques

1) Classical models: ARIMA, exponential smoothing, and state-space models,

2) Machine learning and deep learning: LSTM, TCN, and transformer-based approaches,

3) Handling seasonality, lags, exogenous variables, and forecast evaluation

Chapter 8

Time-Series Forecasting Techniques

You start with the dependable workhorses of time-series forecasting. These methods rely on patterns in the data itself—how current values relate to past values—and they give you clear, interpretable rules you can audit. They're especially useful when you have limited data, want fast results, or need transparent models for explanations.

Step 1 — Check stationarity and prepare the data

Begin by inspecting the data for constant mean and variance over time. If the series drifts or has changing variance, you'll likely need to transform it (for example, differencing or stabilizing the variance with a simple transformation). The goal is to make the data steady enough that simple relationships between past values and future values become predictable. If the series shows seasonality, you'll keep an eye on whether a seasonal component is needed in later steps.

Step 2 — Choose the modeling flavor: ARIMA, SARIMA, or exponential smoothing

ARIMA (AutoRegressive Integrated Moving Average) is a workhorse for nonseasonal data. It uses past values (autoregression), past errors (moving average), and differencing to remove trends. If your data exhibits seasonality, you'll often turn to SARIMA (Seasonal ARIMA), which adds seasonal patterns with additional parameters. Exponential smoothing is another family, including simple, Holt's linear, and Holt-Winters methods. Simple smoothing fits a weighted average of past observations; Holt's methods add a trend term; Holt-Winters adds seasonality. The choice depends on how your data behaves: stable mean with little trend favors smoothing; clear trend or seasonality favors ARIMA/SARIMA or exponential smoothers with seasonal components.

Step 3 — Fit, validate, and compare

Fit the selected model on your training portion of data. Then forecast on a validation set and compare to actuals using a simple forecast-error metric (such as RMSE or MAE). If you have seasonality, check whether the seasonal component aligns well with observed cycles. If accuracy is not satisfactory, revisit the differencing degree (d), the order of AR and MA terms (p and q), or switch to a seasonal variant. State-space formulations give you another path: they provide a probabilistic framework that can be more robust when data arrive irregularly or when you want to naturally include uncertainty in forecasts.

Step 4 — Interpretability and maintenance

One strength of these classical models is clarity. You can explain to a stakeholder why a forecast shifts after a recent holiday or why removing a trend improves predictions. Maintain a lean model menu: a small set of well-understood options that you recheck periodically as data evolve. If the data change shape—new seasonality, structural breaks, or regime changes—you may need to re-estimate or reselect the model quickly.

Examples

Micro-case A: A small shop tracks daily sales for a year and notices a yearly cycle plus a gentle upward drift. You start with Holt-Winters seasonal smoothing. You fit the model, forecast the next two weeks, and see that forecasts track the weekly ups and downs but underreact to a mid-year promotional spike. You add a seasonal component calibrated to the observed cycle and compare performance to a SARIMA model. The two forecasts differ in how they respond to promotions, but the smoothing model remains transparent and fast to recompute each week.

Micro-case B: An energy company records weekly demand with a clear winter peak. You try SARIMA with a seasonal period of 52 weeks and compare it to exponential smoothing with seasonality. The SARIMA fit captures the winter peak more accurately, while smoothing offers quicker run times on a basic setup. Both approaches give you a defensible forecast, and you can explain the difference to the team by pointing to how seasonality is represented in each method.

Exercises

1) Exercise: Take a dataset with monthly sales that shows seasonality. Fit ARIMA or SARIMA and Holt-Winters. Forecast three months ahead. Time: 20–40 minutes. Measure progress by comparing forecast errors on the held-out months and noting which model aligns better with observed peaks.

2) Exercise: For a trend-like series, experiment with first-dDifference and then fit simple ARIMA(1,1,1) and ARIMA(0,1,1). Record whether

differencing improves forecast accuracy. Time: 15–25 minutes. Outcome: choose the model with lower error.

3) Exercise: Add a seasonal component to a nonseasonal ARIMA model and compare performance to a Holt-Winters approach on the same data. Time: 25–40 minutes. Outcome: decide which approach your data favors and document why.

4) Exercise: Create a quick audit sheet listing which model you tried, the chosen parameters, forecast horizon, and the rationale. Time: 10 minutes. Outcome: a reproducible decision log you can reuse.

Troubleshooting

- Problem: The model drifts or overfits in the presence of sudden changes. Quick fix: check for data quality issues, test shorter horizons, and consider a model that can adapt faster (such as a state-space approach or a seasonal smoothing variant with more flexible seasonality).

- Problem: Seasonality is present but not captured. Quick fix: try explicit seasonal terms (SARIMA) or Holt-Winters with a tuned seasonal component; validate against a hold-out period that includes seasonal peaks.

- Problem: Forecast error remains high after differencing. Quick fix: revisit stationarity checks, avoid over-differencing, and consider a model with stronger AR or MA components rather than additional differencing.

- Problem: Data leakage or look-ahead bias slips in. Quick fix: strictly separate training and testing data, and use only past observations to forecast the future.

Tools and templates

- Quick-fit checklist: decide between ARIMA/SARIMA and exponential smoothing based on seasonality and trend; check stationarity; select model; fit; forecast; evaluate; compare; document.

- Parameter-tuning template: p, d, q and P, D, Q with seasonal period S; smoothing parameters for Holt-Winters; clearly note rationale for each choice.

- Audit log: model name, parameters, horizon, validation metric, observed biases, next steps.

Key Takeaway: Classical time-series models give transparent, fast forecasts when seasonality and trends are clear, and they are easy to audit and update.

Coming up next: Model Governance, Ethics, and Regulation

1) Explainability, transparency, and model documentation best practices

2) Detecting bias, ensuring fairness, and protecting consumer rights

3) Regulatory compliance, audit trails, and operational controls

Chapter 9

Model Governance, Ethics, and Regulation

By the end of this chapter you will be able to implement practical governance, ethics, and regulatory practices for AI in finance.

1. Explainability, transparency, and model documentation

You start by making decisions understandable and traceable. Explainability means you can describe, in plain language, why a model makes a certain prediction or decision. Transparency means you share enough information about how the model works and what data it uses so others can see the process, not just the output. Documentation is the written record that keeps all of this organized over time. You build three core habits:

First, create a clear explainability plan for every model. This plan lists who needs to understand the model, what explanations will look like, and when explanations should be provided. It also specifies what counts as a successful explanation for different stakeholders—customers, managers, auditors, and regulators. The plan helps you avoid jargon and translates complex math into simple, actionable reasons.

Second, maintain a simple model card and an audit-ready log. A model card is a compact, human-friendly document that describes the model's purpose, inputs, outputs, limitations, and intended uses. An audit log records decisions about data, features, changes, and test results. It should be easy to follow, time-stamped, and linked to the exact code or dataset versions in use. When someone asks why a loan-denial happened, you can point to the card and logs to explain which inputs influenced the decision and how.

Third, document data lineage and feature origins. You track where data came from, how it was cleaned, and which features were created. This makes it possible to trace a decision back to its data source and to see whether a data change could affect outcomes. Keeping this information simple and current prevents confusion during reviews and helps you spot potential issues early.

Two micro-cases illustrate how this works in practice. Case A: A credit-scoring model in a bank uses a straightforward explanation method that highlights the most influential input factors for each applicant. When a customer asks why they were rated a certain score, you provide a plain-language reason tied to specific inputs, along with a link to the model card and the decision log. Case B: A payments-fraud detector flags a transaction. The analysts receive an explanation that lists the top contributing features and a short rule-based note for why the flag was raised. Both cases show the power of clear explanations paired with robust records.

Key principle: explanations should be usable. If a customer or reviewer cannot understand the reason behind an outcome, the explanation fails its purpose. Build explanations that can be read, not just generated by a machine.

2. Detecting bias, ensuring fairness, and protecting consumer rights

Bias is a risk in any data-driven system. If the data reflect past inequalities or if you rely on proxies for sensitive attributes, outcomes can unfairly favor or harm groups of people. Your job is to anticipate these risks, measure them, and mitigate them without sacrificing performance. You establish a fair-working approach in three steps:

First, audit inputs and outputs for biased patterns. Look for features that could correlate with protected characteristics (like age, race, gender, or location) and check whether outcomes differ meaningfully across groups. Use simple fairness checks that compare results across these groups and ask whether a plan to improve fairness would meaningfully reduce predictive quality. If you see a gap, plan adjustments rather than ignoring it.

Second, apply practical fairness fixes. You can adjust the data or the model so that it treats different groups more equitably. This might mean reweighting samples so underrepresented groups are better learned, rebalancing classes, or removing or replacing problematic features. The aim is to reduce disparate impact while keeping the model performance within acceptable bounds. In many cases, modest adjustments can improve fairness a lot without wrecking accuracy.

Third, protect consumer rights through clear consent and transparent use. Ensure customers know when AI is used to make important financial decisions about them and provide accessible explanations of the factors involved. If a decision has significant consequences, offer a human review option or a clear path to contest the outcome. Fairness isn't just math; it's about respecting people's rights and dignity in financial interactions.

Two micro-cases show bias thinking in action. Case A: A mortgage-eligibility model shows a small but noticeable disparity in approval rates across ZIP codes with different demographics. You adjust by reviewing the data sources, adding representation where needed, and confirming the model doesn't rely on protected proxies. After adjustments, you re-check outcomes and find the gap narrowed without a large loss in predictive power. Case B: A consumer loan-approval model uses a feature that unintentionally correlates with a sensitive attribute. You replace or modify that feature and rerun checks to ensure fairness metrics improve while overall performance stays strong. These examples highlight that fairness work is ongoing, not a one-time fix.

Important note: fairness is contextual. The right balance between fairness and performance depends on the product, the risk level, and regulatory expectations. You document decisions about trade-offs so others can see why certain choices were made. That transparency supports accountability and trust.

3. Regulatory compliance, audit trails, and operational controls

Regulation in finance is about protecting customers and maintaining trust in markets. You align governance with general regulatory expectations by building a clear, repeatable process that covers risk, privacy, auditability, and accountability. You implement three core practices:

First, identify applicable rules and standards. Different financial activities face different requirements, but you typically need to show clear governance, data handling, model validity, and risk management. You gather the relevant guidelines into a single, living checklist you can reference during development and review. This helps you avoid missed steps and keeps your team aligned.

Second, create robust audit trails and change-control processes. Every model version, dataset update, and environment change should leave a trace. You document who approved changes, why they were made, and how validation tests responded. Audit trails make reviews faster and bigger questions easier to answer. They also support regulatory inquiries by showing you followed a disciplined path rather than improvising on the fly.

Third, enforce operational controls and privacy safeguards. You separate duties so no single person can move a model from development to production without checks. You establish data-privacy practices that limit exposure and ensure compliance with privacy laws. You implement basic risk controls like monitoring for unusual activity, regular external and internal reviews, and clearly defined rollback plans in case a model behaves badly in production.

Two micro-cases illustrate these governance patterns. Case A: A fraud-detection model undergoes quarterly audits. The team documents all data sources, feature changes, test results, and the rationale for any policy updates. Regulators can see a structured process and consistent results. Case B: An investment-forecast model runs in production within a controlled API environment. Access to model code and data is restricted, and any production change requires approval, documentation, and backtesting before deployment. The system stays reliable, auditable, and compliant.

Practical notes you can apply now:

- Keep a living governance plan that evolves with your product and regulatory hints. Update it whenever you add a new data source, feature, or use case.

- Build lightweight, human-friendly summaries of your governance work. If you can explain the governance decisions to a curious child, you're likely explaining them well enough for most stakeholders.

- Treat privacy as a first-class design constraint. Don't wait for a regulator to remind you to protect data; bake privacy into how you collect, store, and use information from the start.

Examples and micro-cases are your daily practice field. They reveal how governance, ethics, and regulation come alive, not just how they sound on paper. In a real setting, you'll often juggle trade-offs between transparency, speed, and performance. The right move is to document the reasoning behind each choice and keep the record accessible to everyone who needs it.

Tools, templates, and quick-start resources

- Explainability Report Template: Purpose, Intended Users, Key Explanations, Limitations, Data and Feature Lineage, Change History, and Next Steps.

- Fairness Audit Checklist: Data representativeness, group performance checks, bias-mitigation plan, validation results, and monitoring schedule.

- Audit Trail Log Template: Timestamp, Stakeholders, Change Description, Rationale, Validation Results, and Rollback Plan.

- Data Lineage Diagram Template: Source, Transformation, Feature, Dependents, and Responsible Team.

- Decision Log Snapshot: Decision, Inputs, Outcome, Responsible Person, and Evidence.

Exercises

1) Explainability plan sprint (15–20 minutes). Draft a short explainability plan for a current model. List the key audience, the explanations you will provide, and how you will present them.

Outcome: you can share a ready-to-use explainability plan with stakeholders.

2) Fairness quick audit (15–20 minutes). Take a small, safe dataset or a hypothetical example and perform a quick fairness check across two groups. Note any gaps, potential risks, and a concrete mitigation idea. Outcome: you identify at least one fairness concern and a plan to address it.

3) Audit trail exercise (10–15 minutes). Write a sample audit trail entry for a recent model change, including the reason, approvals, and test results. Outcome: you can produce a clear, regulator-friendly record.

4) Governance skeleton (20–25 minutes). Create a simple governance document skeleton for a new model project, including data handling, change control, and privacy steps. Outcome: you have a reusable governance starter you can adapt.

Troubleshooting

- Problem: Explanations are confusing or overly technical for non-experts.

Fix: Translate explanations into plain-language narratives with everyday examples and avoid technical jargon. Include a short glossary in the model card.

- Problem: Fairness checks show a persistent gap with little room for improvement.

Fix: Revisit data representativeness, consider reweighting or sampling adjustments, and re-run tests. If gaps persist, document the limitation and adjust the use case or thresholds accordingly.

- Problem: Audit trails are incomplete or hard to follow.

Fix: Start logging key events now, even if the model is in earlier stages. Create a simple template and fill it consistently for every change, so reviews become faster over time.

- Problem: Compliance tasks feel heavy or bureaucratic.

Fix: Build a lightweight, repeatable checklist that maps to your actual workflow. Automate where possible (for example, automatic logging of model versions) to keep tasks manageable.

Coming up next: Deployment, Monitoring, and Future Trends

Subtittle: Deployment, Monitoring, and Future Trends

1) Productionizing models: APIs, low-latency inference, and scaling concerns

2) Continuous monitoring, drift detection, and automated retraining

3) Emerging directions: reinforcement learning, federated learning, and synthetic data

Transition: In the next chapter, you will learn how to move your governance-grounded models into production, how to monitor them in real time, and what new directions are shaping the future of AI in finance. You will discover practical steps for building robust APIs, keeping results stable under changing conditions, and exploring new techniques that extend your governance work into live, scalable systems.

Chapter 10

Deployment, Monitoring, and Future Trends

You will be able to deploy AI models in production with reliable APIs, monitor their health and drift, and explore future directions like reinforcement learning, federated learning, and synthetic data in safe, practical ways.

Productionizing models: APIs, low-latency inference, and scaling concerns

When an AI model moves from a test notebook to a live system, you shift from "what the model can do" to "how it behaves under real load." Productionizing means turning the model into a service that others can call, making sure it responds quickly, and keeping it stable as demand grows. The point is to deliver trustworthy, repeatable results every time.

Step 1: Define the API contract and input/output expectations

Decide exactly what data goes into the model and what comes out. Specify data types, units, allowed ranges, and error formats. Agree on what happens when inputs are missing or out of range. The goal is a stable interface that won't break when you update the model. This makes it easier to test, monitor, and onboard new team members.

Step 2: Package the model and choose a serving stack

Package the model with its dependencies in a repeatable way, usually with a container. Pick a serving framework that fits the timing needs: some tasks require very fast, lightweight serving; others can tolerate a bit more latency for richer features. Containerization helps ensure the same environment in development, testing, and production, reducing the “it works on my machine” problem.

Step 3: Optimize for latency and throughput

Real-time decisions need speed. Reduce input size where possible, apply lightweight preprocessing, and consider strategies like batching requests when appropriate. If hardware allows, use lightweight optimization techniques such as quantization or smaller model variants. The idea is to deliver timely results without sacrificing accuracy more than you can afford.

Step 4: Design for scaling and reliability

Make the service stateless so you can spin up more instances when demand grows. Use load balancing to spread work evenly and autoscaling to adapt to traffic—up or down—as needed. Plan for failure with simple fallbacks or circuit breakers, so a single slow or broken component doesn't take everything down. Version your models and have a rollback plan if a new version underperforms.

Two micro-cases

Case A: A payments company deploys a fraud-detection model behind an API gateway. The API accepts transaction data, returns a risk score, and triggers downstream alerts if the score is high. Latency targets are sub-100-millisecond in normal traffic, with a maximum of a few hundred milliseconds during peak times. The engineering team uses containerized serving and implements canary releases so a small percentage of traffic tests the new version before full rollout. Observed benefits include faster decision-making for suspected fraud cases and clearer rollback options when data patterns drift.

Case B: A retail broker runs a nightly batch scoring job for risk reviews. The system processes a large dataset after market close, sends results to downstream dashboards, and stores scores for audit. Reliability is prioritized over ultra-low latency here, but the team still uses a repeatable deployment process and clear logging so issues are easy to pinpoint when the batch run finishes. The example shows that not all AI deployments need live, real-time inference; some still deliver measurable value with scheduled, predictable workloads.

Continuous monitoring, drift detection, and automated retraining

Even well-built models can drift over time as data changes. You need to watch how the model behaves, catch when inputs or trends shift, and have a plan to update the model without disrupting users. Monitoring helps you see problems quickly and keeps your system trustworthy.

Step 5: Implement continuous monitoring of performance and health

Track key signals such as latency, error rates, request volume, and success rates. Add data-focused metrics like distribution of input features and the range of outputs. Centralized logging and metrics dashboards give you a single view of how the service is behaving. Alert thresholds should be simple to understand and actionable—when a metric crosses the threshold, you should know what to do next.

Step 6: Set up drift detection and data quality checks

Drift happens when the data you see in production looks different from the data used to train the model. Simple checks compare current input distributions with historical ones, and monitor the rate of unusual guesses or anomalous outputs. If drift is detected, you may need to pause automated decisions, flag items for human review, or trigger a retraining workflow. Keep alerts clear and avoid noise by tuning sensitivity and combining multiple signals.

Step 7: Build an automated retraining pipeline with governance

Automated retraining means re-running training with fresh data and validating the new model before replacing the old one. Include data verification steps, unit tests for the code and inputs, and performance tests to compare old and new models. Deploy new versions gradually using canary or blue-green strategies, so you can observe impact before a full switch. Keep a clear record of what changed, why, and how it performs in production.

Two more micro-cases

Case C: A bank uses a federated learning setup to update a customer-behavior model without sharing raw data. Local models learn from customers in each region, then share only model updates to refine a global model. The regional data stays in place, supporting privacy and regulatory requirements while still improving overall performance.

Case D: A health-tech firm experiments with synthetic time-series data to augment forecasting tests, helping the team evaluate model responses to rare events without risking real patient data. This practice supports safer experimentation and broader scenario coverage while respecting privacy constraints.

Emerging directions: reinforcement learning, federated learning, and synthetic data

The landscape is always evolving. Some approaches show promise for finance and AI at scale, but they require careful risk assessment and governance. You will not replace solid supervised methods overnight, but you can explore these directions to complement existing workflows where they fit.

Step 8: Reinforcement learning and safe exploration

Reinforcement learning (RL) focuses on learning through interaction with an environment. In finance, RL ideas can help with strategies that adapt over time, but they require strong safety controls. Implement clear boundaries for exploration, define risk limits, and use offline or simulated environments to test before any live deployment. The key is to balance learning with protecting customers and markets from unintended consequences.

Step 9: Federated learning and synthetic data for privacy and coverage

Federated learning lets multiple organizations train a shared model without exchanging raw data. It can improve generalization while protecting sensitive information, but it needs robust privacy safeguards and coordination. Synthetic data, when used responsibly, can expand coverage for rare events or scenarios that aren't well represented in real data. Always validate synthetic data against real-world behavior and document how it's created, what it's protecting, and what it might miss.

Two further micro-cases

Case E: Several regional banks collaborate on a shared risk-model component using federated learning. Each bank trains on its own data, shares updates, and contributes to a stronger, collective model without exposing customer details.

Case F: A trading desk uses synthetic data to stress-test forecasting models against unusual market conditions. This helps reveal blind spots and guide safer parameter choices before touching real funds.

Exercises

1) Deployment map and latency check: Draw or describe your current deployment path from input

to output. Measure approximate latency for a typical request and for peak load. Time: 15 minutes. Progress: you have a baseline to compare against future changes.

2) Monitoring and alert plan: List the core metrics you would monitor, and draft a simple alert rule (e.g., “alert if latency > 200 ms for 5 minutes”). Time: 20 minutes. Progress: a concrete, testable monitoring plan.

3) Drift and retraining plan: Write a short plan that explains when you would trigger a retraining, what data to re-train with, and how you would test the new model before deployment. Time: 25

minutes. Progress: a ready-to-run retraining decision framework.

4) Future directions evaluation: Choose one emerging direction (reinforcement learning, federated learning, or synthetic data). Sketch a small, safe pilot idea that could fit inside your current workflow. Time: 25 minutes. Progress: a concrete pilot concept with potential benefits and caveats.

Troubleshooting: quick fixes for common problems

- Latency is higher than target: reduce input size, enable batching if possible, and check for unnecessary preprocessing. If needed, test a smaller model variant or a lighter serving stack.

- Drift alerts are noisy: tighten thresholds, combine more signals (e.g., both distribution shifts and output anomalies), and ensure alerts require a human review path rather than automatic retraining.

- Retraining fails to deploy: verify the testing suite passes, confirm data versioning is correct, and use a canary deployment to verify behavior before full rollout.

- API failures due to version mismatch: keep a strict versioning policy, maintain backward compatibility windows, and provide clear deprecation notices with transition timelines.

Tools and templates

- Deployment checklist: a one-page list covering API contract, packaging, latency targets, scaling, and rollback plans.

- Monitoring template: a small table with metrics, thresholds, and alert owners.

- Retraining plan template: data sources, training steps, validation tests, deployment steps, and rollback criteria.

- Emergent direction evaluation sheet: a simple pro/con grid for RL, federated learning, and synthetic data, plus a go/no-go decision criteria.

Key Takeaway: Production-ready AI lives at the intersection of stable interfaces, reliable performance, and thoughtful governance. You build for scale, watch for drift, and keep an eye on new ideas that could fit your needs without compromising safety or trust.

Transition: In the next chapter, you will move from how to run AI services to how to measure their impact with real-world performance metrics, and you'll start mapping your own roadmap for continued learning and iteration.

Dear Reader,

Thank you for exploring this series focused on failures and the power of comeback stories. If you find value in these stories and believe in the importance of embracing setbacks as part of growth, we appreciate your support. Please consider sharing a positive review on the platform where you accessed this series.

Your feedback helps spread the message, inspiring more young readers to see challenges as opportunities and to believe in their potential. We understand that mistakes happen, and we thank you for your understanding.

www.ingramcontent.com/pod-product-compliance
Lightning Source LLC
LaVergne TN
LVHW022207200926
848481LV00006B/1878

* 9 7 9 8 2 9 5 5 3 5 5 0 5 *